COOKING CLASS

C•A•K•E•S

COOKBOOK

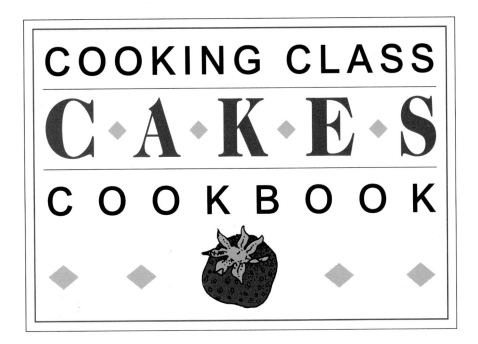

PUBLICATIONS INTERNATIONAL, LTD.

Louis Weber, C.E.O.
Publications International, Ltd.
7373 N. Cicero Ave.
Lincolnwood, IL 60646

Permission is never granted for commercial purposes.

Pyrex is a registered trademark of Corning Incorporated, Corning, NY 14831.

Photography on pages 33 and 65 by Vuksanovich, Chicago.

Remaining photography by Sacco Productions Limited, Chicago.

Pictured on the front cover: Chocolate Sour Cream Cake (*page 47*).
Pictured on the inside front cover: Brandy-Pecan Corn Meal Cake (*page 82*).
Pictured on the back cover: Carrot Cake (*page 26*).

ISBN: 0-7853-0711-7

Manufactured in the U.S.A.

8 7 6 5 4 3 2 1

Microwave Cooking: Microwave ovens vary in wattage. The microwave cooking times given in this publication are approximate. Use the cooking times as guidelines and check for doneness before adding more time. Consult manufacturer's instructions for suitable microwave safe cooking dishes.

The publishers would like to thank the following companies and organizations for the use of their recipes in this publication: Arkansas State Fair; Black Walnut Festival; Celebrate! Kansas Food Recipe Contest; Cherry Marketing Institute; Circleville Pumpkin Festival; Essex Agricultural Society; The Hartford Courant; Illinois State Fair; Michigan Apple Committee; Michigan State Fair; National Date Festival; National Peanut Festival; National Sunflower Association; Nebraska State Fair; New Mexico State Fair; Pollio Dairy Products; The Quaker Oats Company.

CONTENTS

Burnt Sugar Cake (*page 15*)

Black Forest Cake (*page 37*)

Turtle Pecan Cheesecake (*page 88*)

CLASS NOTES

Nothing beats the tantalizing aroma and luscious flavor of a home-baked cake. Whether it's a light, delicate angel food cake or a decadently rich devil's food cake, many of the preparation principles remain the same. The following information on cake basics is sure to provide you with all you'll need to make your next cake presentation one that will win you raves!

CAKE BASICS

Cakes are divided into two categories according to what makes them rise. Butter cakes rely primarily on baking powder or baking soda for height, while sponge cakes depend on the air trapped in the eggs during beating. Some cake recipes specifically call for cake flour, which contains less protein than all-purpose flour and produces a more tender cake.

Butter Cakes

Butter cakes include pound cakes and yellow, white, spice and chocolate layer cakes. These cakes use butter, shortening or oil for moistness and richness and are leavened with baking powder and/or baking soda. Before mixing the batter, soften the butter so that it mixes easily with the sugar.

Sponge Cakes

These cakes achieve their high volume from beaten eggs rather than a leavening agent like baking powder. Sponge cakes do not contain butter, oil or shortening. Angel food cakes are the most popular and are literally fat free since they use only egg whites, not yolks. Yellow sponge cakes are prepared with whole eggs. Chiffon cakes are also lightened with beaten eggs, but they are not true sponge cakes because they contain vegetable oil. When preparing sponge cakes, be sure to beat the eggs to the proper stage; do not overbeat or underbeat them. Handle the beaten eggs gently when folding them into the other ingredients or they will lose air and volume.

PREPARING PANS

Always use the exact pan size called for in the recipe. If the pan is too large, the cake will not rise properly or brown evenly. If the pan is too small, the cake will sink in the center and the texture will be coarse; the batter may also run over the top of the pan during baking.

For butter cakes, use shiny metal pans or pans with a nonstick finish. Grease and flour the pans before mixing the cake batter so that the cake can be baked immediately. To grease and flour cake pans, use a pastry brush, paper towel or waxed paper to apply a thin, even layer of shortening. Sprinkle flour into the greased pan; shake or tilt the pan to coat evenly with flour, then tap lightly to remove any excess. To line pans with paper, invert pan; top with waxed paper. Press around the edge of the pan to form a crease in paper. Cut along crease to form a circle. Grease the pan, but *do not* flour it. Press the paper onto the bottom of the greased pan.

Sponge cakes are usually baked in tube pans. The center tube helps the heat circulate during baking and also supports the delicate structure of the cake. *Do not* grease the pans for sponge cakes. The ungreased pan lets the batter cling to the sides as it rises.

BAKING

Place the filled cake pan(s) in the center of a preheated oven. Oven racks may need to be set lower for cakes baked in tube pans. If two racks are used, arrange them so they divide the oven into thirds and then stagger the pans so they are not directly over each other. Avoid opening the oven door during the first half of the baking time. The oven temperature must remain constant in order for the cake to rise properly.

A butter cake is done when it begins to pull away from the sides of the pan, the top springs back when lightly touched and a cake tester or wooden pick inserted in the center comes out clean and dry. A sponge cake is done when it is delicately browned and the top springs back when lightly touched.

COOLING

After removing butter cakes from the oven, let them stand in their pans on wire racks for 10 minutes, or as the recipe directs. Run a knife around the edge of the cake to loosen it from the sides of the pan. Place a wire rack, top-side down, over the pan. Flip the rack and the pan over together and the cake should drop out onto the rack. If it does not come out, tap the bottom of the pan; the cake should come out easily. Remove the pan. Remove the paper liner from the cake if one was used. Place a second wire rack over the cake and flip both racks and the cake back over so the cake can cool top-side up. Remove the top rack.

Invert a sponge cake baked in a tube pan onto a heatproof funnel or bottle immediately after removing it from the oven. If it is cooled top side up, it will fall. Do not remove a sponge cake from the pan until it is completely cool.

FROSTING

Make sure the cake is completely cool before frosting it. Brush off any loose crumbs from the cake's surface. To keep the cake plate clean, place small strips of waxed paper under the edges of the cake; remove them after the cake has been frosted. You will achieve a more professional look if you first apply a layer of frosting thinned with milk on the cake as a base coat to help seal in any remaining crumbs. Let this base coat dry a few minutes before covering with the final frosting. For best results, use a flat metal spatula for applying frosting. Place a mound of frosting in the center of the cake. Spread frosting across the top by pushing it out toward the sides with the spatula. Always keep the spatula on a frosted surface, because once it touches the cake surface, crumbs will mix in with the frosting. To frost sides, work from the top down, making sure the spatula only touches frosting.

STORING

Store one-layer cakes in their baking pans, tightly covered. Store two- or three-layer cakes in a cake-saver or under a large inverted bowl. If the cake has a fluffy or cooked frosting, insert a teaspoon handle under the edge of the cover to prevent an airtight seal and moisture buildup. Cakes with whipped cream frostings or cream fillings should be stored in the refrigerator. Unfrosted cakes can be frozen for up to 4 months if well wrapped in plastic. Thaw in their wrappers at room temperature. Frosted cakes should be frozen unwrapped until the frosting hardens, and then wrapped and sealed; freeze for up to 2 months. To thaw, remove the wrapping and thaw at room temperature or in the refrigerator. Cakes with fruit or custard fillings do not freeze well because they become soggy when thawed.

Chiffon Cake

5 eggs
¹/₂ teaspoon cream of tartar
2¹/₄ cups sifted all-purpose flour
1¹/₂ cups sugar
1 tablespoon baking powder
1 teaspoon salt
³/₄ cup water
¹/₂ cup vegetable oil
1 teaspoon vanilla
1 teaspoon almond extract
Strawberries, kiwifruit, star fruit, orange and whipped cream for garnish

1. Preheat oven to 325°F.

2. To separate egg yolk from white, gently tap egg in center against a hard surface, such as side of bowl. Holding shell half in each hand, gently transfer yolk back and forth between 2 shell halves. Allow white to drip down between 2 halves into medium bowl.

3. When all white has dripped into bowl, place yolk in another bowl. Transfer white to third bowl. Repeat with remaining 4 eggs. (Egg whites must be free from any egg yolk to reach the proper volume when beaten.)

4. Add cream of tartar to egg whites. Beat with electric mixer at high speed until stiff peaks form. At this stage, stiff peaks remain on surface, and mixture does not slide when bowl is tilted. Set aside.

5. Sift together dry ingredients into large bowl. Make a well in flour mixture.

6. Add egg yolks; mix well. Blend in water, oil and flavorings.

7. Fold egg whites into egg yolk mixture with rubber spatula by gently cutting down to bottom of bowl, scraping up side of bowl, then folding over top of mixture. Repeat until egg whites are evenly incorporated. Pour into ungreased 10-inch tube pan.

8. Bake 55 minutes. *Increase oven temperature to 350°F.* Continue baking 10 minutes or until cake springs back when lightly touched with finger.

9. Invert pan; place on top of clean empty bottle. Allow cake to cool completely in pan. Garnish, if desired.

Makes one 10-inch tube cake

Step 2. Separating egg yolk from white.

Step 5. Sifting together dry ingredients.

Step 7. Folding in egg white mixture.

Cherry-Pineapple Upside-Down Cake

1¼ cups sifted cake flour
2 teaspoons baking powder
¼ teaspoon salt
½ cup (1 stick) butter or
    margarine, softened, divided
¾ cup granulated sugar
1 egg
½ cup milk
1 teaspoon vanilla
¾ cup packed brown sugar
1 can (20 ounces) crushed
    pineapple, well drained
1 can (16 ounces) sour pie
    cherries, drained
    Fresh mint leaves for garnish

1. Preheat oven to 350°F.

2. Combine flour, baking powder and salt in medium bowl; set aside.

3. Beat together ¼ cup butter and granulated sugar in large bowl with electric mixer at high speed until light and fluffy.

4. Blend in egg. Add flour mixture alternately with milk, beating well after each addition. Blend in vanilla.

5. Melt remaining ¼ cup butter in 9-inch ovenproof skillet or 9-inch round cake pan. Stir in brown sugar. If necessary, tilt skillet to evenly cover bottom of skillet with brown sugar mixture.

6. Top brown sugar mixture with pineapple.

7. Reserve a few cherries for garnish, if desired. Spoon remaining cherries over pineapple; top with batter.

8. Bake 50 minutes or until wooden pick inserted in center comes out clean.

9. Remove cake from oven. Cool cake in pan on wire rack 10 minutes. Loosen edges and turn upside down onto cake plate. Garnish, if desired. *Makes one 9-inch cake*

Step 5. Tilting skillet to cover bottom of skillet with brown sugar mixture.

Step 7. Spooning cherries over pineapple.

Step 9. Removing cake from oven.

Sweet Zucchini Spice Cake

3 cups grated peeled zucchini
(about 1 pound)
1 cup ground walnuts
1 cup flaked coconut
4 eggs
1 cup vegetable oil
2 tablespoons vanilla
2½ cups granulated sugar
3 cups all-purpose flour
2 teaspoons ground cinnamon
1½ teaspoons baking soda
1 teaspoon baking powder
1 teaspoon salt
**Pineapple Cream Cheese Icing
(page 14)**

1. Preheat oven to 350°F. Grease bottoms and sides of two 10-inch round cake pans with small amount of shortening.

2. Add 2 to 3 teaspoons flour to *each* pan. Gently tap side of pan to evenly coat bottom and side with flour. Invert pan and gently tap bottom to remove excess flour.

3. Combine zucchini, walnuts and coconut in medium bowl; set aside.

4. Beat together eggs, oil and vanilla in large bowl with electric mixer at medium speed until well blended. Beat in granulated sugar. Gradually add combined dry ingredients, mixing well after each addition. Stir in zucchini mixture. Pour evenly into prepared pans.

5. Bake 35 to 40 minutes or until wooden pick inserted in centers comes out clean. Cool layers in pans on wire racks 10 minutes. Loosen edge of cake with knife or flexible metal spatula. Using oven mitts or hot pads, place wire cooling rack on top of cake in pan. Turn cake and pan over so wire rack is on bottom. Gently shake cake to release from pan. Remove pan. Repeat with remaining cake layers. Cool layers completely.

continued on page 14

Step 1. Greasing the pan.

Step 2. Flouring the pan.

Sweet Zucchini Spice Cake, continued

6. Gently brush loose crumbs off tops and sides of cake layers with pastry brush or hands.

7. Prepare Pineapple Cream Cheese Icing. Fill and frost cake with icing.

Makes one 2-layer cake

Pineapple Cream Cheese Icing

1 package (8 ounces) cream cheese
1 pound (about 4½ cups) powdered sugar
½ cup (1 stick) margarine, softened
1 can (8 ounces) crushed pineapple, drained

1. Place cream cheese on opened package on cutting board. With utility knife, cut cream cheese lengthwise into ½-inch slices. Then cut crosswise into ½-inch pieces. Let stand at room temperature until softened. (Cream cheese will be easy to push down.)

2. Sift powdered sugar into large bowl with sifter or fine-meshed sieve.

3. Beat together cream cheese and margarine in another large bowl with electric mixer at high speed until creamy. Blend in pineapple.

4. Gradually add powdered sugar, beating until frosting is smooth and of spreading consistency.

Step 6. Brushing off crumbs before icing.

Pineapple Cream Cheese Icing: Step 1. Softening cream cheese.

Pineapple Cream Cheese Icing: Step 2. Sifting powdered sugar.

Burnt Sugar Cake

1½ cups granulated sugar, divided
½ cup boiling water
2 eggs
½ cup (1 stick) margarine, softened
1 teaspoon vanilla
2¼ cups all-purpose flour
1 tablespoon baking powder
1 teaspoon salt
1 cup milk
Caramel Frosting (page 16)
Caramelized Sugar Shapes for garnish (page 16)

1. Heat ½ cup granulated sugar in heavy 8-inch skillet over medium heat, stirring constantly, until sugar is melted and golden brown.

2. *Reduce heat to low.* Gradually stir boiling water into sugar mixture; continue cooking until sugar is dissolved, stirring constantly.

3. Preheat oven to 375°F. Grease and flour two 8-inch round cake pans. (Technique on page 12.)

4. To separate egg yolk from white, gently tap egg in center against a hard surface, such as side of bowl. Holding shell half in each hand, gently transfer yolk back and forth between 2 shell halves. Allow white to drip down between 2 halves into medium bowl.

5. When all white has dripped into bowl, place yolk in another bowl. Transfer white to third bowl. Repeat with remaining egg. (Egg whites must be free from any egg yolk to reach the proper volume when beaten.)

6. Beat egg whites with electric mixer at medium speed until foamy.

7. Gradually add ½ cup granulated sugar, beating at high speed until stiff peaks form; set aside. (Technique on page 40.)

8. Beat together margarine and remaining ½ cup granulated sugar in large bowl until light and fluffy. Beat in egg yolks. Blend in vanilla. Gradually add sugar syrup, mixing until well blended.

continued on page 16

Step 1. Melting sugar.

Step 2. Adding water to sugar mixture.

Step 4. Separating egg yolk from white.

Burnt Sugar Cake, continued

9. Add combined dry ingredients to margarine mixture alternately with milk, beating well after each addition. Fold in egg white mixture. (Technique on page 8.) Pour batter evenly into prepared pans.

10. Bake 20 to 25 minutes or until wooden pick inserted in centers comes out clean. Cool layers in pans on wire racks 10 minutes.

11. Loosen edges of cakes with knife or spreader. Using oven mitts or hot pads, place wire cooling rack on top of cake and pan. Turn cake over so wire rack is on bottom. Gently shake cake to release from pan. Remove pan. Repeat with remaining cake layer. Cool layers completely.

12. Gently brush loose crumbs off tops and sides of cake layers with pastry brush or hands.

13. To assemble, place one cake layer on cake plate. Tuck small strips of waxed paper under cake to keep plate clean while frosting cake. Prepare Caramel Frosting. Spread top of layer with frosting.

14. Top bottom layer with remaining cake layer. Frost top and side with remaining frosting. Remove waxed paper strips. Garnish, if desired.

Makes one 2-layer cake

Caramel Frosting

   2 tablespoons margarine
   ²⁄₃ cup packed brown sugar
   ¹⁄₈ teaspoon salt
   ¹⁄₃ cup evaporated milk
   2¹⁄₂ cups powdered sugar
   ¹⁄₂ teaspoon vanilla

1. Melt margarine in 2-quart saucepan. Stir in brown sugar, salt and evaporated milk. Bring to a boil, stirring constantly. Remove from heat; cool to lukewarm.

2. Beat in powdered sugar with electric mixer at high speed until frosting is of spreading consistency. Blend in vanilla.

Caramelized Sugar Shapes: Heat ¹⁄₂ to ³⁄₄ cup granulated sugar in heavy 8-inch skillet over medium heat, stirring constantly, until sugar is melted and golden brown. Immediately drizzle into desired shapes on greased cookie sheet. Let stand until set. Carefully remove from cookie sheet.

Step 11. Removing cake layer from pan.

Step 13. Spreading Caramel Frosting.

Buttermilk Pound Cake

3 cups sifted all-purpose flour
¹/₂ teaspoon baking powder
¹/₂ teaspoon baking soda
¹/₂ teaspoon salt
1 cup (2 sticks) butter or margarine, softened
2 cups superfine sugar
2 eggs
1 teaspoon vanilla
1 teaspoon lemon extract
1 cup buttermilk
1 orange for garnish
Starfruit slices and strawberry slices for garnish

1. Preheat oven to 350°F. Grease two 9 × 5-inch loaf pans with small amount of shortening. Add 2 to 3 teaspoons flour to *each* pan. Gently tap side of pan to evenly coat bottom and sides with flour. Invert pan and gently tap bottom to remove excess flour.

2. Combine flour, baking powder, baking soda and salt in medium bowl; set aside.

3. Beat together butter and sugar in large bowl with electric mixer at high speed until light and fluffy. Add eggs, 1 at a time, beating well after each addition. Blend in vanilla and lemon extract.

4. Add flour mixture alternately with buttermilk, beating well after each addition. Pour evenly into prepared pans.

5. Bake 35 to 40 minutes or until wooden pick inserted in centers comes out clean.

6. Remove thin strips of peel from orange using citrus zester. Use as garnish.

7. Cool loaves in pans on wire racks 10 minutes. Loosen edges; remove to racks to cool completely. Garnish, if desired.

Makes two 9 × 5-inch loaves

Step 1. Flouring the pan.

Step 3. Adding eggs.

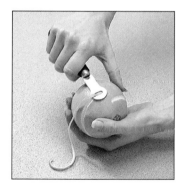

Step 6. Removing peel from orange.

Boston Cream Pie

½ cup shortening
1 cup granulated sugar
1 egg
1 teaspoon vanilla
1¼ cups all-purpose flour
1½ teaspoons baking powder
½ teaspoon salt
¾ cup milk
 Custard Filling (page 22)
 Chocolate Glaze (page 22)

1. Preheat oven to 350°F. Grease and flour one 9-inch round cake pan. (Technique on page 12.)

2. Beat together shortening and sugar in large bowl with electric mixer at medium speed until well blended. Blend in egg and vanilla. Add combined dry ingredients alternately with milk, beating well after each addition. Pour into prepared pan.

3. Bake 35 minutes or until wooden pick inserted in center comes out clean. Cool cake in pan 10 minutes. Loosen edge of cake with knife or flexible metal spatula. Using oven mitts or hot pads, place wire cooling rack on top of cake in pan. Turn cake and pan over so wire rack is on bottom. Gently shake cake to release from pan. Remove pan. Cool completely.

4. Use ruler to measure height of cake layer. Insert wooden picks halfway up side of cake layer at 2-inch intervals.

5. To split layer in half, place 15- to 18-inch length of thread at far side of cake. Pull ends of thread together through cake, following line at top of wooden picks.

6. Prepare Custard Filling; set aside. Prepare Chocolate Glaze; set aside.

7. To assemble, place bottom half of cake on cake plate; brush off loose crumbs with hands or pastry brush. Spread cake layer with filling.

continued on page 22

Step 4. Using ruler to measure height of cake layer.

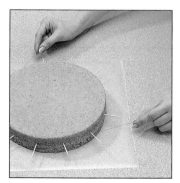

Step 5. Splitting cake layer in half.

Step 7. Spreading cake layer with Custard Filling.

8. Cover with top half of cake layer. Spread top with glaze. Refrigerate until glaze is completely set. Store in refrigerator.   *Makes one 9-inch cake*

Custard Filling

   ⅓ **cup granulated sugar**
   2 tablespoons cornstarch
   ¼ **teaspoon salt**
1½ **cups milk**
   2 egg yolks, slightly beaten
   2 teaspoons vanilla

1. Combine granulated sugar, cornstarch and salt in 2-quart saucepan. Gradually stir in milk.

2. Cook over medium heat, stirring constantly, until mixture thickens and comes to a boil. Boil 1 minute, stirring constantly.

3. Gradually stir small amount of hot mixture into egg yolks; mix thoroughly.

4. Return egg yolk mixture to hot mixture in pan. Return to a boil; boil 1 minute, stirring constantly. *(Do not overcook.)*

5. Remove saucepan from heat; stir in vanilla. Cool to room temperature. Refrigerate.

Chocolate Glaze

   2 squares (1 ounce each) unsweetened chocolate
   3 tablespoons butter
   1 cup powdered sugar
   ¾ **teaspoon vanilla**
   1 to 2 tablespoons hot water

1. Combine chocolate and butter in medium saucepan; stir over low heat until melted. Remove from heat.

2. Stir in powdered sugar and vanilla. Stir in water, a teaspoonful at a time, until glaze is of desired consistency. Cool slightly.

Custard Filling: Step 2. Cooking until mixture thickens.

Custard Filling: Step 3. Adding small amount of hot mixture into egg yolks.

Chocolate Glaze: Step 1. Melting chocolate and butter.

White Buttermilk Cake

6 eggs
3 cups sifted cake flour
1 teaspoon baking soda
½ teaspoon salt
1 cup shortening
2 cups granulated sugar, divided
1 cup buttermilk
2 teaspoons clear vanilla
½ teaspoon almond extract
1 teaspoon cream of tartar
Creamy Frosting (page 24)

1. Preheat oven to 350°F. Grease and flour two 9-inch or three 8-inch round cake pans. (Technique on page 12.)

2. To separate egg white from yolk, gently tap egg in center against a hard surface, such as side of bowl. Holding shell half in each hand, gently transfer yolk back and forth between 2 shell halves. Allow white to drip down between 2 halves into bowl.

3. When all white has dripped into bowl, place yolk in another bowl. Transfer white to third bowl. Repeat with remaining 5 eggs. (Egg whites must be free from any egg yolk to reach the proper volume when beaten.) Store unused egg yolks, covered with water, in airtight container. Refrigerate for up to 2 to 3 days.

4. Combine flour, baking soda and salt in medium bowl; set aside.

5. Beat together shortening with 1⅓ cups granulated sugar in large bowl with electric mixer at medium speed until light and fluffy. Add flour mixture alternately with buttermilk, beating well after each addition. Blend in vanilla and almond extract.

6. Beat egg whites in separate bowl with electric mixer at medium speed until foamy. Add cream of tartar; beat at high speed until soft peaks form.

7. Gradually add remaining ⅔ cup granulated sugar, beating until stiff peaks form. (Technique on page 40.)

Step 2. Separating egg white from yolk.

Step 6. Beating egg whites until soft peaks form.

continued on page 24

White Buttermilk Cake, *continued*

8. Stir small amount of egg whites into batter. Fold batter into remaining egg whites with rubber spatula by gently cutting down to bottom of bowl, scraping up side of bowl, then folding over top of mixture. Repeat until batter is evenly incorporated.

9. Pour batter evenly into prepared pans.

10. Bake 30 to 35 minutes or until wooden pick inserted in centers comes out clean. Cool layers in pans on wire racks 10 minutes. Loosen edge of cake with knife or flexible metal spatula. Using oven mitts or hot pads, place wire cooling rack on top of cake in pan. Turn cake and pan over so wire rack is on bottom. Gently shake cake to release from pan. Remove pan. Repeat with remaining cake layers. Cool layers completely.

11. Gently brush loose crumbs off tops and sides of cake layers with pastry brush or hands.

12. Prepare Creamy Frosting. Fill and frost cake.

Makes one 2- or 3-layer cake

Creamy Frosting

3 tablespoons all-purpose flour
1 cup milk
1 cup (2 sticks) butter, softened
1 cup powdered sugar
1 teaspoon vanilla

1. Combine flour and milk in medium saucepan; stir over low heat until thickened. Cool.

2. Beat butter in large bowl with electric mixer at medium speed until creamy. Add powdered sugar; beat until fluffy. Blend in vanilla.

3. Add milk mixture; beat until thick and smooth.

Step 10. Removing cakes to rack to cool.

Creamy Frosting: Step 3. Adding milk mixture.

Carrot Cake

³/₄ **pound carrots**
1 **cup granulated sugar**
1 **cup packed brown sugar**
1 **cup vegetable oil**
1 **cup Polly-O® Ricotta Cheese**
3 **eggs**
2 **cups all-purpose flour**
2 **teaspoons baking powder**
2 **teaspoons baking soda**
1 **teaspoon salt**
2 **teaspoons ground cinnamon**
¹/₂ **teaspoon ground nutmeg**
¹/₄ **to ¹/₂ cup raisins**
¹/₂ **cup chopped pineapple***
¹/₂ **cup chopped walnuts**
    Cream Cheese Topping
    (page 28)
    Additional raisins and chopped
    walnuts for garnish

*If using canned pineapple, use drained unsweetened pineapple.

1. Preheat oven to 350°F. Grease 10-inch tube pan with small amount of shortening.

2. Add 2 to 3 teaspoons flour to pan; gently tap side of pan to evenly coat bottom and side with flour. Invert pan and tap bottom to remove excess flour.

3. Trim ends of carrots; discard. Peel carrots. Shred with shredding disk of food processor or hand shredder. Measure 2 cups; set aside.

4. Beat together sugars, oil and ricotta cheese in large bowl with electric mixer at medium speed until well blended.

5. Add eggs, 1 at a time, beating well after each addition.

6. Sift together dry ingredients; gradually add to sugar mixture, mixing until well blended.

7. To prevent raisins from sinking in batter, add small amount of flour to raisins in small bowl; toss lightly to coat.

8. Add raisins to batter with carrots, pineapple and walnuts; mix well.

continued on page 28

Step 1. Greasing tube pan.

Step 3. Shredding carrots.

Step 8. Adding raisins, carrots, pineapple and walnuts to batter.

Carrot Cake, *continued*

9. Pour batter into prepared pan, spreading evenly to edge.

10. Bake 1 hour or until wooden pick inserted in center comes out clean.

11. Cool cake in pan on wire rack 10 minutes. Loosen edges and remove to rack to cool completely. Refrigerate.

12. Prepare Cream Cheese Topping. Spread over cake just before serving. Garnish, if desired.

Makes one 10-inch tube cake

Cream Cheese Topping

2 tablespoons butter, softened
4 ounces cream cheese, softened
$^1/_2$ cup Polly-O® Ricotta Cheese
1 teaspoon vanilla
2 cups powdered sugar

1. Beat together butter, cream cheese, ricotta cheese and vanilla in large bowl with electric mixer at medium speed until well blended.

2. Add powdered sugar; beat until smooth and creamy. Add additional powdered sugar, if necessary, for desired consistency.

Step 9. Pouring batter into pan.

Step 10. Testing cake for doneness with wooden pick.

Cream Cheese Topping: Step 1. Beating together butter, cream cheese, ricotta cheese and vanilla.

Lady Baltimore Cake

1¼ cups shortening
2¼ cups sugar
  2 teaspoons vanilla
3¼ cups all-purpose flour
4½ teaspoons baking powder
1½ teaspoons salt
1½ cups milk
  8 egg whites
    Fruit Filling (page 30)
    Fluffy Frosting (page 30)

1. Preheat oven to 350°F. Grease three 9-inch round cake pans with small amount of shortening.

2. Invert pan onto work surface. Place sheet of waxed paper over bottom of pan. Press around entire edge of pan to form crease in waxed paper. Cut along crease with scissors to form 9-inch circle. Repeat to make three circles. Place one circle in bottom of each pan.

3. Beat together shortening and sugar in large bowl with electric mixer at high speed until light and fluffy. Blend in vanilla.

4. Sift together dry ingredients. Add to sugar mixture alternately with milk, beating well after each addition.

5. Beat egg whites in separate bowl with electric mixer at high speed until stiff peaks form. (Technique on page 40.)

6. Fold egg whites into batter with rubber spatula by gently cutting down to bottom of bowl, scraping up side of bowl, then folding over top of mixture. Repeat until egg whites are evenly incorporated. Pour evenly into prepared pans.

7. Bake 30 minutes or until wooden pick inserted in centers comes out clean. Cool layers in pans on wire racks 10 minutes. Loosen edge of cake with knife or flexible metal spatula. Using oven mitts or hot pads, place wire cooling rack on top of cake in pan. Turn cake and pan over so wire rack is on bottom. Gently shake cake to release from pan. Remove pan. Repeat with remaining cake layers. Cool layers completely.

Step 2. Pressing around edge of pan to form crease.

Step 3. Beating together shortening and sugar.

continued on page 30

Lady Baltimore Cake, continued

8. Gently brush loose crumbs off tops and sides of cake layers with pastry brush or hands.

9. Prepare Fruit Filling. To assemble, spread two cake layers with filling; stack on cake plate. Top with remaining cake layer.

10. Prepare Fluffy Frosting. Frost cake with frosting.

Makes one 3-layer cake

Fruit Filling

¹/₂ cup (1 stick) butter or margarine
1 cup sugar
¹/₂ cup water
¹/₃ cup bourbon or brandy*
10 egg yolks, slightly beaten
1 cup finely chopped raisins
³/₄ cup chopped pecans
¹/₂ cup drained chopped maraschino
   cherries
¹/₂ cup flaked coconut
³/₄ teaspoon vanilla

*Bourbon may be omitted. Increase water to ³/₄ cup. Add 1 tablespoon rum extract with vanilla.

1. Melt butter in 2-quart saucepan. Stir in sugar, water and bourbon. Bring to a boil over medium-high heat, stirring occasionally to dissolve sugar.

2. Stir small amount of hot mixture into egg yolks.

3. Add egg yolk mixture to remaining hot mixture in saucepan.

4. Cook until thickened; remove from heat.

5. Stir in raisins, pecans, cherries and coconut. Blend in vanilla. Cool completely.

Fluffy Frosting

1¹/₂ cups sugar
¹/₂ cup water
2 egg whites**
2 teaspoons corn syrup *or* ¹/₄ teaspoon
   cream of tartar
   Dash of salt
1 teaspoon vanilla

**Use clean, uncracked eggs.

1. Combine sugar, water, egg whites, corn syrup and salt in top of double boiler. Beat with electric mixer at high speed 30 seconds.

2. Place on top of range; cook, stirring occasionally, over simmering water 7 minutes.

3. Remove from heat; add vanilla. Beat with electric mixer at high speed 3 minutes or until frosting is of spreading consistency.

Fruit Filling: Step 4. Cooking until thickened.

Fluffy Frosting: Step 1. Beating sugar mixture for 30 seconds.

Fluffy Frosting: Step 3. Beating to spreading consistency.

Angel Food Cake

1¼ cups cake flour
1⅓ cups *plus* ½ cup sugar, divided
12 egg whites
1¼ teaspoons cream of tartar
¼ teaspoon salt
1 teaspoon vanilla
¼ teaspoon almond extract
   Fresh strawberries for serving
   (optional)

1. Preheat oven to 350°F.

2. Sift together flour with ½ cup sugar four times.

3. Beat egg whites with cream of tartar, salt, vanilla and almond extract in large bowl with electric mixer at high speed until stiff peaks form. (Technique on page 40.)

4. Gradually add remaining 1⅓ cups sugar, beating well after each addition. Fold in flour mixture with rubber spatula by gently cutting down to bottom of bowl, scraping up side of bowl, then folding over top of mixture. Repeat until flour mixture is evenly incorporated.

5. Pour into ungreased 10-inch tube pan.

6. Bake 35 to 40 minutes or until cake springs back when lightly touched with finger.

7. Invert pan; place on top of clean empty heatproof bottle. Allow cake to cool completely in pan before removing from pan.

8. Serve with strawberries, if desired.

Makes one 10-inch tube cake

Step 2. Sifting together flour and sugar.

Step 4. Folding in flour mixture.

Step 6. Testing for doneness.

Elegant Chocolate Log

3¼ cups sifted powdered sugar, divided
5 tablespoons sifted all-purpose flour
½ teaspoon salt
5 tablespoons unsweetened cocoa
6 eggs
¼ teaspoon cream of tartar
1¼ teaspoons vanilla
1 tablespoon water
1 square (1 ounce) unsweetened chocolate
12 large marshmallows *or* ¾ cup miniature marshmallows
1 cup whipping cream
2 tablespoons granulated sugar
3 to 4 tablespoons light cream
¼ cup chopped pecans

1. Preheat oven to 375°F. Grease 15 × 10 × 1-inch jelly-roll pan with small amount of shortening; line with waxed paper.

2. Sift together 1¾ cups powdered sugar, flour, salt and cocoa three times; set aside.

3. To separate egg yolk from white, gently tap egg in center against a hard surface, such as side of bowl. Holding shell half in each hand, gently transfer yolk back and forth between 2 shell halves. Allow white to drip down between 2 halves into bowl.

4. When all white has dripped into bowl, place yolk in another bowl. Transfer white to third bowl. Repeat with remaining 5 eggs. (Egg whites must be free from any egg yolk to reach the proper volume when beaten.)

5. Beat egg whites in large bowl with electric mixer at high speed until foamy. Add cream of tartar; beat until stiff peaks form. (Technique on page 40.) Set aside.

6. Beat egg yolks in separate large bowl with electric mixer at high speed until thick and lemon colored.

7. Blend in vanilla and water. Add dry ingredients; beat on medium speed until well blended. Fold in egg whites with rubber spatula by gently cutting down to bottom of bowl, scraping up side of bowl, then folding over top of mixture. Repeat until egg whites are evenly incorporated.

8. Spread batter into prepared pan.

continued on page 36

Step 1. Greasing the pan.

Step 3. Separating egg yolk from white.

Step 6. Beating egg yolks until thick and lemon colored.

Elegant Chocolate Log, continued

9. Bake 15 to 20 minutes or until wooden pick inserted in center comes out clean. Meanwhile, lightly dust clean dish towel with additional powdered sugar.

10. Loosen warm cake from edges of pan with spatula; invert onto prepared towel. Remove pan; carefully peel off paper.

11. Roll up cake gently, from one short end, by folding cake over and then tucking it in towel.

12. Continue rolling cake, using towel as an aid.

13. Let cake cool completely in towel on wire rack.

14. Meanwhile, unwrap chocolate; place chocolate in small heavy saucepan over *very low* heat, stirring constantly, until chocolate is just melted. (Or, place *unwrapped* chocolate in small microwavable dish. Microwave on HIGH (100% power) 1 to 2 minutes or until almost melted, stirring after each minute. Stir until smooth.) Set aside to cool.

15. If using large marshmallows, cut into smaller pieces with scissors or knife. (To prevent sticking, occasionally dip scissors or knife into small amount of cornstarch before cutting.)

16. Beat whipping cream in separate small bowl with electric mixer at high speed until thickened. Gradually add granulated sugar, beating until soft peaks form. Fold in marshmallows with rubber spatula by gently cutting down to bottom of bowl, scraping up side of bowl, then folding over top of mixture. Repeat until marshmallows are evenly incorporated.

17. Unroll cake; remove towel.

18. Spread cake with whipped cream mixture; reroll cake.

19. Combine cooled chocolate and remaining 1½ cups powdered sugar in small bowl. Stir in light cream, 1 tablespoonful at a time, until frosting is of spreading consistency. Spread on cake roll. Sprinkle cake with pecans. Refrigerate.

Makes one jelly-roll cake

Step 11. Rolling up the cake.

Step 18. Rerolling cake after spreading with whipped cream mixture.

Step 19. Spreading frosting on cake roll.

Black Forest Cake

2 cups *plus* 2 tablespoons
   all-purpose flour
1½ teaspoons baking powder
¾ teaspoon baking soda
¾ teaspoon salt
2 cups granulated sugar
¾ cup unsweetened cocoa
3 eggs
1 cup milk
½ cup vegetable oil
1 tablespoon vanilla
   Cherry Topping (page 38)
   Whipped Cream Frosting
   (page 38)

1. Preheat oven to 350°F. Grease and flour two 9-inch round cake pans with small amount of shortening. Line bottoms with waxed paper. (Technique on page 29.)

2. Combine flour, baking powder, baking soda, salt, sugar and cocoa in large bowl. Add eggs, milk, oil and vanilla; beat with electric mixer at medium speed until well blended. Pour evenly into prepared pans.

3. Bake 35 minutes or until wooden pick inserted in centers comes out clean. Cool layers in pans on wire racks 10 minutes. Loosen edge of cake with knife or flexible metal spatula. Using oven mitts or hot pads, place wire cooling rack on top of cake in pan. Turn cake and pan over so wire rack is on bottom. Gently shake cake to release from pan. Remove pan. Repeat with remaining cake layer. Cool layers completely.

4. While cake is baking, prepare Cherry Topping; set aside to cool.

5. Use ruler to measure height of each cake layer; insert wooden picks halfway up side of layer at 2-inch intervals.

6. With long serrated knife, split each cake layer horizontally in half, cutting along line marked with wooden picks.

7. Tear one split layer into crumbs; set aside.

8. Prepare Whipped Cream Frosting. Reserve 1½ cups for decorating cake; set aside.

continued on page 38

Step 1. Lining bottoms of pans with waxed paper.

Step 5. Measuring height of cake layer.

Step 6. Cutting cake layer in half.

Black Forest Cake, continued

9. Gently brush loose crumbs off top and side of each cake layer with pastry brush or hands.

10. To assemble, place one cake layer on cake plate. Spread with 1 cup Whipped Cream Frosting; top with ¾ cup Cherry Topping. Top with second cake layer; repeat layers of frosting and topping. Top with third cake layer.

11. Frost side of cake with remaining frosting. Gently press reserved crumbs onto frosting on side of cake.

12. Spoon reserved frosting into pastry bag fitted with star decorator tip. Pipe around top and bottom edges of cake. Spoon remaining topping onto top of cake. *Makes one 3-layer cake*

Cherry Topping

2 cans (20 ounces each) tart pitted cherries, undrained
1 cup granulated sugar
¼ cup cornstarch
1 teaspoon vanilla

Drain cherries, reserving ½ cup juice. Combine reserved juice, cherries, sugar and cornstarch in 2-quart saucepan. Cook over low heat until thickened, stirring constantly. Stir in 1 teaspoon vanilla. Cool; set aside.

Whipped Cream Frosting

3 cups whipping cream
⅓ cup powdered sugar

Chill large bowl and beaters thoroughly. Combine chilled whipping cream and powdered sugar in chilled bowl. Beat with electric mixer at high speed until stiff peaks form. To test, lift beaters from whipped cream; stiff peaks should remain on surface.

Step 11. Pressing reserved crumbs onto side of cake.

Step 12. Piping frosting on edges of cake.

Chocolate Angel Food Cake

1½ **cups granulated sugar, divided**
¾ **cup sifted cake flour**
¼ **cup cocoa**
¼ **teaspoon salt**
12 **egg whites**
1½ **teaspoons cream of tartar**
1½ **teaspoons vanilla**
 Powdered sugar and frosting
  daisies* for garnish

*To make frosting daisies, gradually add 1 to 2 teaspoons milk to small amount of powdered sugar, mixing until well blended (frosting should have slightly stiff consistency). Tint with food coloring, if desired. Spoon into pastry bag fitted with star decorator tip. Pipe onto cake.

1. Preheat oven to 375°F.

2. Sift together ¾ cup granulated sugar with flour, cocoa and salt two times; set aside.

3. Beat egg whites in large bowl with electric mixer at medium speed until foamy.

4. Add cream of tartar; beat at high speed until soft peaks form.

5. Gradually add remaining ¾ cup granulated sugar, 2 tablespoons at a time, beating until stiff peaks form. At this stage, stiff peaks should remain on surface, and mixture does not slide when bowl is tilted. Blend in vanilla.

6. Sift about ¼ of the cocoa mixture over egg white mixture.

7. Fold cocoa mixture into batter. Repeat with remaining cocoa mixture. (Technique on page 8.) Pour into ungreased 10-inch tube pan.

8. Bake 35 to 40 minutes or until cake springs back when lightly touched with finger.

9. Invert pan; place on top of clean empty heatproof bottle. Allow cake to cool completely before removing from pan.

10. Turn cake onto cake plate. Dust lightly with powdered sugar, if desired.

11. Decorate with frosting daisies, if desired.
Makes one 10-inch tube cake

Step 5. Testing egg white mixture for stiff peaks.

Step 9. Inverting pan to allow cake to cool.

*Piping frosting daisies.

Zucchini Chocolate Cake

2 to 3 medium zucchini
¹/₂ cup (1 stick) margarine or butter, softened
¹/₂ cup vegetable oil
1²/₃ cups granulated sugar
2 eggs
1 teaspoon vanilla
¹/₂ teaspoon chocolate flavoring
2¹/₂ cups all-purpose flour
¹/₄ cup unsweetened cocoa
1 teaspoon baking soda
¹/₂ teaspoon salt
¹/₂ cup buttermilk
¹/₂ cup chopped nuts
1 package (6 ounces) semisweet chocolate chips

1. Preheat oven to 325°F. Grease 13 × 9-inch baking pan with small amount of shortening.

2. Add 3 to 4 teaspoons flour to pan; gently tap side of pan to evenly coat bottom and sides with flour. Invert pan and gently tap bottom to remove excess flour.

3. Shred zucchini using bell grater or hand-held grater; measure 2 cups. Set aside. (No need to peel zucchini before shredding.)

4. Beat together margarine, oil and sugar in large bowl with electric mixer at medium speed until well blended.

5. Add eggs, 1 at a time, beating well after each addition. Blend in vanilla and chocolate flavoring.

6. Combine flour, cocoa, baking soda and salt in medium bowl. Add to margarine mixture alternately with buttermilk, beating well after each addition. Stir in zucchini.

7. Pour into prepared pan. Sprinkle with nuts and chocolate chips.

8. Bake 55 minutes or until wooden pick inserted in center comes out clean; cool cake completely in pan on wire rack. Cut into squares. Frost with your favorite chocolate frosting, if desired.

Makes one 13 × 9-inch cake

Step 1. Greasing the pan.

Step 3. Shredding zucchini.

Step 7. Sprinkling nuts and chocolate chips over batter.

Tin Roof Sundae Cake

1 cup (2 sticks) butter, softened
2 cups granulated sugar
4 eggs
3 cups all-purpose flour
2 teaspoons baking powder
1 cup milk
1 teaspoon vanilla
1 teaspoon butter flavoring
3 tablespoons unsweetened cocoa
  Peanut Filling (page 46)
  Chocolate Cream Frosting
  (page 46)
1 bar (2 ounces) white chocolate
  for garnish

1. Preheat oven to 350°F. Grease three 8- or 9-inch round cake pans with small amount of shortening.

2. Add 2 to 3 teaspoons flour to *each* pan. Gently tap side of pan to evenly coat bottom and side with flour. Invert pan and gently tap bottom to remove excess flour.

3. Beat together butter and sugar in large bowl with electric mixer at high speed until light and fluffy.

4. Add eggs, 1 at a time, beating well after each addition.

5. Combine flour and baking powder in medium bowl. Add to butter mixture alternately with milk, beating well after each addition. Blend in vanilla and butter flavoring.

6. Pour ⅓ of the batter into each of two of the prepared pans.

7. Blend cocoa into the remaining batter; pour into remaining pan.

8. Bake 30 minutes or until wooden pick inserted in centers comes out clean.

9. Cool layers in pans on wire racks 10 minutes. Loosen edge of cake with knife or flexible metal spatula. Using oven mitts or hot pads, place wire cooling rack on top of cake in pan. Turn cake and pan over so wire rack is on bottom. Gently shake cake to release from pan. Remove pan. Repeat with remaining layers. Cool layers completely.

10. Gently brush loose crumbs off tops and sides of cake layers with pastry brush or hands.

Step 2. Flouring the pan.

Step 6. Pouring batter into two of the pans.

Step 10. Brushing crumbs from cake layers.

continued on page 46

Tin Roof Sundae Cake, continued

11. Prepare Peanut Filling and Chocolate Cream Frosting. To assemble, place one yellow layer on cake plate; spread with ¹/₂ of the filling.

12. Cover with chocolate layer; spread with remaining filling.

13. Top with remaining yellow cake layer. Frost with Chocolate Cream Frosting.

14. Unwrap white chocolate; place chocolate in small heavy saucepan. Heat over *very low* heat, stirring constantly, just until chocolate is melted. (Or, place *unwrapped* chocolate square in microwavable dish. Microwave on HIGH (100% power) 1 to 2 minutes or until almost melted, stirring after each minute. Stir until smooth.) Cool slightly.

15. Spoon chocolate into pastry bag fitted with writing tip. Pipe onto cake.

Makes one 3-layer cake

Peanut Filling

¹/₂ cup (1 stick) butter, softened
4 ounces cream cheese, softened
2 cups powdered sugar
³/₄ cup crunchy peanut butter
1 teaspoon vanilla
1 teaspoon butter flavoring
¹/₃ cup finely chopped peanuts
1 to 2 tablespoons milk (optional)

1. Beat together butter and cream cheese in medium bowl with electric mixer at medium speed until creamy.

2. Gradually add powdered sugar, beating until fluffy.

3. Blend in peanut butter, vanilla and butter flavoring. Stir in peanuts. Add milk if necessary for desired consistency.

Chocolate Cream Frosting

2 squares (1 ounce each) unsweetened chocolate
4 ounces cream cheese, softened
¹/₄ cup (¹/₂ stick) butter, softened
3 tablespoons whipping cream
1 tablespoon lemon juice
1 teaspoon vanilla
2 cups powdered sugar

1. Melt chocolate (see step 14 for directions). Set aside to cool.

2. Beat together cream cheese and butter in medium bowl with electric mixer at medium speed until creamy. Beat in whipping cream. Blend in chocolate, lemon juice and vanilla.

3. Gradually beat in powdered sugar until mixture is fluffy.

Step 12. Spreading remaining Peanut Filling.

Step 15. Piping white chocolate onto cake.

Chocolate Cream Frosting: Step 3. Beating in powdered sugar.

Chocolate Sour Cream Cake

½ cup boiling water
½ cup unsweetened cocoa
⅔ cup butter or margarine, softened
1¾ cups granulated sugar
2 eggs
1 teaspoon vanilla
2½ cups sifted cake flour
1½ teaspoons baking soda
½ teaspoon salt
1 cup sour cream
    Cocoa-Nut Filling (page 48)
    Fluffy Cocoa Frosting
    (page 48)
1 square (1 ounce) unsweetened chocolate for garnish
    Chocolate-Dipped Strawberries (page 48) and fresh mint leaves for garnish

1. Preheat oven to 350°F. Grease two 9-inch round cake pans with small amount of shortening.

2. Add 2 to 3 teaspoons flour to *each* pan. Gently tap side of pan to evenly coat bottom and side with flour. Invert pan and gently tap bottom to remove excess flour.

3. Gradually add boiling water to cocoa in small bowl, stirring until well blended; cool slightly.

4. Meanwhile, beat butter and sugar in large bowl with electric mixer at high speed until well blended.

5. Add eggs, 1 at a time, beating well after each addition. Blend in vanilla.

6. Combine flour, baking soda and salt in medium bowl. Add to butter mixture alternately with sour cream, beating well after each addition.

7. Add cocoa mixture to batter; beat until well blended.

8. Pour batter evenly into prepared pans.

9. Bake 35 minutes or until wooden pick inserted in centers comes out clean. Cool layers in pans on wire racks 10 minutes. Loosen edge of cake with knife or flexible metal spatula. Using oven mitts or hot pads, place wire cooling rack on top of cake in pan. Turn cake and pan over so wire rack is on bottom. Gently shake cake to release from pan. Remove pan. Repeat with remaining cake layer. Cool layers completely.

Step 2. Flouring the pan.

Step 5. Adding eggs.

Step 7. Adding cocoa mixture to batter.

continued on page 48

10. Gently brush loose crumbs off tops and sides of cake layers with pastry brush or hands.

11. Prepare Cocoa-Nut Filling and Fluffy Cocoa Frosting. To assemble, place one cake layer on cake plate; spread with Cocoa-Nut Filling.

12. Top with second cake layer. Frost with Fluffy Cocoa Frosting.

13. Grate chocolate; sprinkle over cake.

14. Prepare Chocolate-Dipped Strawberries. Place on cake. Surround with mint leaves, if desired.

Makes one 2-layer cake

Cocoa-Nut Filling

¹/₂ cup Fluffy Cocoa Frosting (recipe follows)
¹/₄ cup flaked coconut (optional)
¹/₄ cup chopped nuts, toasted

Combine ingredients in small bowl; mix until well blended.

Fluffy Cocoa Frosting

4¹/₂ cups powdered sugar
¹/₂ cup unsweetened cocoa
¹/₂ cup (1 stick) butter or margarine, softened
5 tablespoons half-and-half or milk
1 teaspoon vanilla

1. Combine powdered sugar and cocoa in medium bowl; set aside.

2. Beat butter in large bowl with electric mixer at medium speed until creamy.

3. Add ¹/₂ of cocoa mixture; beat until fluffy. Blend in half-and-half and vanilla.

4. Gradually add remaining cocoa mixture, beating until frosting is of spreading consistency.

Chocolate-Dipped Strawberries

¹/₂ cup semisweet chocolate chips
1 teaspoon shortening
10 to 12 fresh strawberries, cleaned

1. Place chocolate chips and shortening in small microwavable bowl. Microwave on HIGH (100% power) 1¹/₂ to 3 minutes or until smooth when stirred, stirring after each minute. (Or, place in top of double boiler. Heat over boiling water until chocolate is smooth when stirred.)

2. Dip strawberries into chocolate. Place on waxed paper-lined jelly-roll pan or cookie sheet; let stand until chocolate is set.

Step 11. Spreading cake layer with Cocoa-Nut Filling.

Step 13. Grating chocolate.

Chocolate-Dipped Strawberries: Step 2. Dipping strawberries into chocolate.

Date Torte

**Chocolate Nut Filling
(page 52)**
**½ pound pitted dates (about
1 cup)**
9 egg whites
2 cups sifted powdered sugar
2 cups coarsely ground almonds
2 tablespoons dry bread crumbs
**Additional powdered sugar for
garnish**

1. Prepare Chocolate Nut Filling; refrigerate until ready to use.

2. Preheat oven to 350°F. Grease two 9-inch round cake pans with small amount of shortening. Add 2 to 3 teaspoons flour to *each* pan. Gently tap side of pan to evenly coat bottom and side with flour. Invert pan and gently tap bottom to remove excess flour.

3. Reserve a few dates for garnish, if desired; cut up remaining dates with lightly floured scissors or sharp knife.

4. Beat egg whites in large bowl with electric mixer at medium speed until foamy. Gradually add sugar, beating at high speed until stiff peaks form. At this stage, stiff peaks remain on surface, and mixture does not slide when bowl is tilted.

5. Combine almonds and bread crumbs; fold into egg white mixture with rubber spatula by gently cutting down to bottom of bowl, scraping up side of bowl, then folding over top of mixture. Repeat until evenly incorporated. Fold in chopped dates. Pour evenly into prepared pans.

6. Bake 25 to 30 minutes or until lightly browned. Cool layers in pans on wire racks 10 minutes. Loosen edge of cake with knife or flexible metal spatula. Using oven mitts or hot pads, place wire cooling rack on top of cake in pan. Turn cake and pan over so wire rack is on bottom. Gently shake cake to release from pan. Remove pan. Repeat with remaining cake layer. Cool layers completely.

continued on page 52

Step 2. Flouring the pan.

Step 3. Cutting up dates.

Step 4. Testing egg whites for stiff peaks.

Date Torte, continued

7. Gently brush loose crumbs off tops and sides of cake layers with pastry brush or hands.

8. To assemble, place one layer on cake plate; spread with filling. Cover with second cake layer.

9. Place paper doily on top of cake. Dust with powdered sugar; remove doily.

10. Place reserved dates between two sheets of waxed paper. Flatten with rolling pin.

11. Remove waxed paper. Cut dates into desired shape with sharp knife or shaped cutter; place on top of cake.

Makes one 2-layer cake

Chocolate Nut Filling

**1 square (1 ounce) semisweet
   chocolate, coarsely chopped
$^{1}/_{2}$ cup (1 stick) butter, softened
1 cup sifted powdered sugar
$^{1}/_{2}$ cup coarsely ground almonds**

1. Place chocolate in 1-cup glass measure. Microwave at HIGH (100% power) 2 to 3 minutes or until chocolate is melted, stirring after 1 minute; set aside.

2. Beat together butter and powdered sugar in medium bowl with electric mixer at medium speed until light and fluffy.

3. Blend in melted chocolate. Stir in almonds.

Step 9. Dusting cake with powdered sugar.

Chocolate Nut Filling:
Step 1. Melting chocolate.

Banana Cake

2½ cups all-purpose flour
1 teaspoon salt
¾ teaspoon baking powder
¾ teaspoon baking soda
2 to 3 ripe bananas
⅔ cup shortening
1⅔ cups sugar
2 eggs
⅔ cup buttermilk, divided
⅔ cup chopped walnuts
  Vanilla Frosting (page 54)
  Banana slices and fresh mint
    leaves for garnish

1. Preheat oven to 375°F. Grease two 9-inch round cake pans with small amount of shortening. Add 2 to 3 teaspoons flour to *each* pan. Gently tap side of pan to evenly coat bottom and side with flour. Invert pan and gently tap bottom to remove excess flour.

2. Combine flour, salt, baking powder and baking soda in medium bowl; set aside.

3. Peel bananas and place in medium bowl. Mash with fork. Measure 1¼ cups; set aside.

4. Beat together shortening and sugar in large bowl with electric mixer at medium speed until light and fluffy. Add eggs, 1 at a time, beating well after each addition.

5. Stir in mashed bananas. Add flour mixture alternately with buttermilk, beating well after each addition. Stir in walnuts. Pour evenly into prepared pans.

6. Bake 30 to 35 minutes or until wooden pick inserted in centers comes out clean. Cool layers in pans on wire racks 10 minutes.

continued on page 54

Step 1. Flouring the pan.

Step 4. Adding eggs.

Step 5. Adding bananas.

Banana Cake, continued

7. Loosen edge of cake with knife or flexible metal spatula. Using oven mitts or hot pads, place wire cooling rack on top of cake in pan. Turn cake and pan over so wire rack is on bottom. Gently shake cake to release from pan. Remove pan. Repeat with remaining cake layer. Cool layers completely.

8. Gently brush loose crumbs off tops and sides of cake layers with pastry brush or hands.

9. Prepare Vanilla Frosting. To assemble, place one cake layer on plate; spread with some of frosting. Cover with second cake layer.

10. Frost top and side of cake with frosting. Use flexible metal spatula to make surface as smooth as possible.

11. Pull cake comb around sides and top of cake for ridged effect. Garnish, if desired.   *Makes one 2-layer cake*

Vanilla Frosting

$^{1}/_{3}$ cup *plus* 2 tablespoons all-purpose
    flour
    Dash of salt
  1 cup milk
$^{1}/_{2}$ cup shortening
$^{1}/_{2}$ cup (1 stick) margarine, softened
1$^{1}/_{4}$ cups granulated sugar
  1 teaspoon vanilla

1. Combine flour and salt in 2-quart saucepan. Gradually stir in milk until well blended. Cook over medium heat until thickened, stirring constantly. Cool.

2. Beat together shortening and margarine in large bowl with electric mixer at medium speed until creamy. Add sugar; beat until light and fluffy. Blend in vanilla. Add cooled flour mixture; beat until smooth.

Step 7. Removing cake layer from pan.

Step 11. Pulling cake comb across cake.

Apple Upside-Down Cake

¼ cup (½ stick) *plus*
   3 tablespoons butter, divided
½ cup packed brown sugar
½ teaspoon ground cinnamon
¼ teaspoon ground nutmeg
¼ teaspoon ground mace
3 McIntosh apples*
2 teaspoons lemon juice
1⅓ cups sifted cake flour
¾ cup granulated sugar
1¾ teaspoons baking powder
¼ teaspoon salt
½ cup milk
1 teaspoon vanilla
1 egg, separated (technique on
   page 8)

*Substitute any large cooking apples for McIntosh apples.

1. Preheat oven to 375°F.

2. Melt ¼ cup butter in 8-inch square baking pan. Add brown sugar and spices; mix well.

3. Peel apples. Remove cores; discard.

4. Cut apples into rings. Arrange over brown sugar mixture in bottom of pan; sprinkle with lemon juice. Set aside.

5. Combine cake flour, granulated sugar, baking powder and salt in large bowl. Cut in remaining 3 tablespoons butter with pastry blender until mixture resembles coarse crumbs.

6. Add milk and vanilla; beat with electric mixer at low speed until dry ingredients are moistened. Continue beating 2 minutes at medium speed. Blend in egg yolk.

7. Clean beaters of electric mixer. Beat egg white in small bowl with electric mixer at high speed until stiff peaks form. (Technique on page 40.) Gently fold egg whites into batter. Pour over apples in pan.

8. Bake 35 minutes or until wooden pick inserted in center comes out clean. Cool cake in pan on wire rack 5 minutes. Loosen edges and invert onto serving plate. Let stand 1 minute before removing pan. Serve warm.

Makes one 8-inch square cake

Step 3. Removing cores of apples.

Step 5. Cutting in butter.

Spanish Orange-Almond Cake

1 medium orange
1/3 cup shortening
1 cup *plus* 2 tablespoons sugar, divided
1 egg
1 1/4 cups all-purpose flour
1 1/2 teaspoons baking powder
1/2 teaspoon salt
3/4 cup milk
1/2 cup sliced almonds
1/4 cup orange-flavored liqueur
Additional orange for garnish

1. Preheat oven to 350°F. Grease and flour 8-inch square or 9-inch round cake pan. (Technique on page 53.)

2. Finely grate colored portion of orange peel using bell grater or hand-held grater. Measure 4 teaspoons orange peel; set aside.

3. Beat together shortening and 1 cup sugar in large bowl with electric mixer at medium speed until light and fluffy. Add egg; beat until well blended.

4. Combine flour, baking powder and salt in medium bowl. Add to sugar mixture alternately with milk, beating well after each addition. Stir in orange peel. Pour into prepared pan; sprinkle with almonds.

5. Bake 40 to 45 minutes or until wooden pick inserted in center comes out clean.

6. Sprinkle with remaining 2 tablespoons sugar; drizzle with liqueur.

7. Cool cake in pan on wire rack 10 minutes. Loosen edge of cake with knife or flexible metal spatula. Using oven mitts or hot pads, place wire cooling rack on top of cake in pan. Turn cake and pan over so wire rack is on bottom. Gently shake cake to release from pan. Remove pan. Cool almond side up.

8. If desired, use citrus zester to remove colored peel, not white pith, of additional orange; sprinkle over top of cake.

Makes one 8- or 9-inch cake

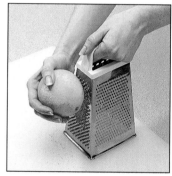

Step 2. Grating orange peel.

Step 4. Sprinkling batter with almonds.

Step 6. Drizzling cake with liqueur.

Fresh Pear Cake

4 cups chopped peeled pears
2 cups granulated sugar
1 cup chopped nuts
3 cups all-purpose flour
2 teaspoons baking soda
1/2 teaspoon salt
1/2 teaspoon ground cinnamon
1/2 teaspoon ground nutmeg
2 eggs
1 cup vegetable oil
1 teaspoon vanilla
    Powdered sugar for garnish

1. Preheat oven to 375°F. Grease 10-inch fluted tube or tube pan with small amount of shortening.

2. Add 2 to 3 teaspoons flour to pan. Gently tap side of pan to evenly coat bottom, side, and center cone with flour. Invert pan and gently tap bottom to remove excess flour.

3. Combine pears, granulated sugar and nuts in medium bowl; mix lightly. Let stand 1 hour, stirring frequently.

4. Combine flour, baking soda, salt, cinnamon and nutmeg in separate medium bowl; set aside.

5. Beat eggs in large bowl with electric mixer at medium speed. Blend in oil and vanilla. Add flour mixture; mix well. Add pear mixture; stir well. Pour into prepared pan.

6. Bake 1 hour and 15 minutes or until wooden pick inserted in center comes out clean. Cool cake in pan on wire rack 10 minutes. Loosen edges and remove to rack to cool completely. (Technique on page 12.)

7. Place cake on cake plate. Insert strips of waxed paper under cake to keep plate clean.

8. Dust lightly with powdered sugar. Remove waxed paper.

Makes one 10-inch tube cake

Step 1. Greasing fluted tube pan.

Step 6. Loosening edges of cake.

Step 7. Inserting strips of waxed paper under cake.

Sunflower Lemon Cake

2 lemons
1½ cups sugar
1 cup sunflower oil
6 eggs
1⅔ cups *plus* 1 tablespoon
  all-purpose flour, divided
2 teaspoons baking powder
¼ teaspoon salt
½ cup sunflower kernels
  Lemon Twist Garnish*
  **Whipped cream, lemon peel
  and fresh mint leaves for
  garnish**

***Lemon Twist Garnish:** Cut lemon into slices, each about ¼ inch thick. Make one cut in each slice from center to outer edge; twist slice.

1. Preheat oven to 300°F. Grease two 9×5-inch loaf pans with small amount of shortening.

2. Add 2 to 3 teaspoons flour to *each* pan. Gently tap side of pan to evenly coat bottom and sides with flour. Invert pan and tap bottom to remove excess flour.

3. Finely grate colored portion of lemon peel using bell grater or hand-held grater. Measure 5 teaspoons.

4. Beat together sugar, lemon peel and oil in large bowl with electric mixer at medium speed. Add eggs, 1 at a time, beating well after each addition.

5. Add 1⅔ cups flour, baking powder and salt; mix well.

6. Combine remaining 1 tablespoon flour and sunflower kernels in small bowl; toss lightly. Stir into batter.

7. Pour batter evenly into prepared pans.

8. Bake 1 hour or until wooden pick inserted in centers comes out clean. Cool loaves in pans on wire racks 10 minutes. Loosen edges; remove to racks to cool completely. Garnish, if desired. *Makes two 9×5-inch loaves*

Step 2. Flouring the pan.

Step 6. Tossing sunflower kernels with flour.

*Lemon Twist Garnish: Making lemon twists.

Punch Bowl Cake

1 package (18.25 ounces) butter cake mix with pudding *plus* ingredients to prepare mix

1 package (5.1 ounces) vanilla flavor instant pudding and pie filling mix *plus* ingredients to prepare mix

2 cans (21 ounces each) cherry pie filling, divided

1 can (20 ounces) crushed pineapple, undrained, divided

1 container (12 ounces) frozen whipped topping, thawed, divided

½ cup chopped nuts, divided

1. Prepare and bake cake mix according to package directions for 13 × 9-inch cake; cool completely.

2. Prepare pudding mix according to package directions.

3. Crumble ½ of the cake into bottom of large bowl. (A small punch bowl works well.)

4. Cover with ½ of the pudding.

5. If desired, reserve a few cherries from one can of cherry pie filling for garnish. Top pudding with layers of ½ each of the pineapple, remaining cherry pie filling and whipped topping. Sprinkle with ½ of the nuts.

6. Repeat layers, using remaining cake, pudding, pineapple and cherry pie filling.

7. Top with remaining nuts and whipped topping. Garnish with reserved cherries.

Makes one cake

Step 3. Crumbling cake into large bowl.

Step 4. Covering cake with ½ of the pudding.

Step 6. Topping with cherry pie filling.

Peaches and Oats Cake

½ cup chopped pecans
1 can (16 ounces) sliced peaches
1 package (8 ounces) cream cheese, softened
¾ cup packed brown sugar
¼ cup granulated sugar
4 eggs, beaten
½ cup milk
1 teaspoon vanilla
1 cup gingersnap crumbs
1 cup almond brickle bits
½ cup rolled oats
Whipped cream, additional peach slices and fresh mint leaves for garnish

1. Preheat oven to 350°F. Grease 9-inch square baking pan with small amount of shortening.

2. Place pecans in shallow baking pan. Bake 10 to 12 minutes or until lightly toasted, stirring occasionally. Remove from oven; leave oven on for cake. Set pecans aside to cool.

3. Drain peaches. Coarsely chop peaches and let stand on paper towels until ready to use.

4. Beat together cream cheese, brown sugar and granulated sugar in large bowl with electric mixer at medium speed until well blended.

5. Add eggs, 1 at a time, beating well after each addition. Blend in milk and vanilla. Stir in pecans, crumbs, brickle bits and oats.

6. Stir peaches into cream cheese mixture; pour into prepared pan.

7. Bake 40 to 45 minutes or until center is firm and edges are golden brown. Serve warm or chilled. Garnish, if desired.

Makes one 9-inch cake

Step 2. Toasting pecans.

Step 5. Stirring in pecans, crumbs, brickle bits and oats.

Step 6. Stirring in peaches.

Blueberry Cake

1 lemon
¹/₂ cup (1 stick) butter, softened
²/₃ cup sugar, divided
1 egg
2¹/₂ teaspoons vanilla, divided
1¹/₂ cups all-purpose flour
1¹/₂ teaspoons baking powder
4 cups fresh blueberries
2 cups sour cream
2 egg yolks
¹/₄ teaspoon ground cardamom
Lemon peel and fresh mint leaves for garnish

1. Preheat oven to 350°F. Grease 9-inch springform pan with small amount of shortening.

2. Finely grate colored portion of lemon peel using bell grater or hand-held grater. Measure ¹/₄ teaspoon. Set aside.

3. Beat together butter and ¹/₃ cup sugar in large bowl with electric mixer at medium speed until light and fluffy. Blend in egg and 1¹/₂ teaspoons vanilla.

4. Combine flour and baking powder in medium bowl. Add to butter mixture, mixing until well blended. Spread onto bottom of prepared pan; cover with blueberries.

5. Combine remaining ¹/₃ cup sugar, 1 teaspoon vanilla, sour cream, egg yolks, cardamom and lemon peel; pour over blueberries.

6. Bake 50 to 55 minutes or until set. *(Do not overbake.)* Cool 10 minutes. Loosen rim of pan. Cool cake completely before removing rim of pan. Garnish, if desired.

Makes one 9-inch cake

Step 4. Covering batter with blueberries.

Step 5. Pouring sour cream mixture over blueberries.

Step 6. Loosening rim of pan.

Apple-Nut Cinnamon Streusel Cake

4 **eggs**
2 **cups granulated sugar**
2 **cups sour cream**
3 **cups all-purpose flour**
1 **teaspoon baking powder**
1 **teaspoon baking soda**
¼ **teaspoon salt**
1½ **cups peeled chopped apples**
½ **cup sunflower kernels, toasted***
    Sunflower Topping (recipe follows)
    Whipped cream and additional toasted sunflower kernels for garnish

* To toast sunflower kernels, spread in single layer on baking sheet. Bake in 275°F oven, stirring occasionally, until golden brown.

1. Preheat oven to 350°F. Grease 13 × 9-inch baking pan.

2. Beat together eggs, sugar and sour cream in large bowl with electric mixer at medium speed until well blended.

3. Combine flour, baking powder, baking soda and salt in medium bowl. Add to sugar mixture; mix well. Stir in apples and sunflower kernels.

4. Pour batter into prepared pan. Prepare Sunflower Topping. Sprinkle on top of batter.

5. Bake 25 to 30 minutes or until wooden pick inserted in center comes out clean. Serve warm or at room temperature. Garnish, if desired. *Makes one 13 × 9-inch cake*

Sunflower Topping

¼ **cup sunflower margarine, softened**
⅔ **cup packed brown sugar****
⅔ **cup all-purpose flour**
½ **teaspoon ground cinnamon**
½ **cup sunflower kernels**

**To correctly measure brown sugar, spoon sugar into ⅓ cup dry measure. Pack into cup with back of spoon until sugar is level with top of cup. Repeat.

1. Combine margarine and brown sugar in medium bowl; mix until well blended.

2. Add flour and cinnamon, mix well. Stir in sunflower kernels.

Step 3. Stirring in apples.

Step 4. Sprinkling with Sunflower Topping.

**Measuring brown sugar.

Fruit Cake

3 cups chopped walnuts or pecans
2 packages (4 ounces each)
  candied pineapple
1 package (8 ounces each)
  candied cherries
1 package (8 ounces) chopped
  dates
³/₄ cup sifted all-purpose flour
³/₄ cup sugar
¹/₂ teaspoon baking powder
¹/₂ teaspoon salt
3 eggs, slightly beaten
1 teaspoon vanilla

1. Preheat oven to 300°F. Line 9 × 5-inch loaf pan with greased waxed paper.

2. Stir together nuts, pineapple, cherries and dates in large bowl; set aside.

3. Combine flour, sugar, baking powder and salt in medium bowl. Sift over nut mixture.

4. Lightly toss flour mixture with nut mixture until well coated.

5. Blend in eggs and vanilla. Spread into prepared pan.

6. Bake 1 hour and 45 minutes or until golden brown. Cool completely in pan on wire rack before removing from pan.

Makes one 9 × 5-inch loaf

Step 1. Lining pan with waxed paper.

Step 3. Sifting flour mixture over nut mixture.

Step 4. Tossing until nut mixture is well coated.

Sour Cream Coffeecake Cupcakes

1 cup (2 sticks) butter, softened (*do not use margarine*)
2 cups *plus* 4 teaspoons sugar, divided
2 eggs
1 cup sour cream
1 teaspoon vanilla
2 cups all-purpose flour
1 teaspoon salt
$\frac{1}{2}$ teaspoon baking soda
1 cup chopped black walnuts
1 teaspoon ground cinnamon

1. Preheat oven to 350°F. Insert paper liners into 18 muffin cups.

2. Beat together butter and 2 cups sugar in large bowl with electric mixer at medium speed. Add eggs, 1 at a time, beating well after each addition. Blend in sour cream and vanilla.

3. Combine flour, salt and baking soda in medium bowl. Add to butter mixture; mix well.

4. Stir together remaining 4 teaspoons sugar, walnuts and cinnamon in small bowl.

5. Fill prepared muffin cups $\frac{1}{3}$ full with batter; sprinkle with $\frac{2}{3}$ of the walnut mixture.

6. Cover with remaining batter. Sprinkle with remaining walnut mixture.

7. Bake 25 to 30 minutes or until wooden pick inserted into centers comes out clean. Remove cupcakes from pan; cool on wire rack.

Makes 1½ dozen cupcakes

Step 1. Lining muffin cups with paper liners.

Step 5. Sprinkling with walnut mixture.

Step 6. Covering with remaining batter.

Velvety Coconut and Spice Cake

Granulated sugar
2½ cups all-purpose flour
1½ teaspoons baking powder
¾ teaspoon baking soda
½ teaspoon salt
1½ teaspoons ground cinnamon
¼ teaspoon ground cloves
¼ teaspoon ground nutmeg
¼ teaspoon ground allspice
¼ teaspoon ground cardamom
½ cup (1 stick) butter or margarine, softened
½ cup packed brown sugar
4 eggs
1 teaspoon vanilla
1½ cups light cream
¼ cup molasses
1½ cups shredded coconut
⅔ cup orange marmalade
Creamy Orange Frosting (page 78)
Candied Orange Rose (page 78) and toasted coconut for garnish

1. Preheat oven to 350°F. Grease three 8-inch round cake pans; sprinkle with enough granulated sugar to lightly coat bottoms and sides of pans.

2. Combine flour, baking powder, baking soda, salt and spices in medium bowl; set aside.

3. Beat butter in large bowl with electric mixer at medium speed until creamy.

4. Add ½ cup granulated sugar and brown sugar; beat until light and fluffy.

5. Add eggs, 1 at a time, beating well after each addition. Blend in vanilla.

6. Combine light cream and molasses in small bowl. Add flour mixture to egg mixture alternately with molasses mixture, beating well after each addition.

7. Stir in coconut; pour evenly into prepared pans.

8. Bake 20 minutes or until wooden pick inserted in centers comes out clean. Cool layers in pans on wire racks 10 minutes. Loosen edge of cake with knife or flexible metal spatula. Using oven mitts or hot pads, place wire cooling rack on top of cake in pan. Turn cake and pan over so wire rack is on bottom. Gently shake cake to release from pan. Repeat with remaining cake layers. Cool layers completely.

continued on page 78

Step 4. Beating in sugars until light and fluffy.

Step 6. Adding molasses mixture.

Step 7. Stirring in coconut.

Velvety Coconut and Spice Cake, continued

9. Gently brush loose crumbs off tops and sides of cake layers with pastry brush or hands.

10. To assemble, spread two cake layers with marmalade; stack on cake plate. Top with third layer.

11. Prepare Creamy Orange Frosting. Frost top and side of cake. Refrigerate. Garnish, if desired.

Makes one 3-layer cake

Creamy Orange Frosting

  1 package (3 ounces) cream cheese, softened
  2 cups sifted powdered sugar
  Few drops orange extract
  Milk (optional)

1. Beat cream cheese in large bowl until creamy. Gradually add powdered sugar, beating until fluffy. Blend in orange extract.

2. If necessary, add milk, 1 teaspoonful at a time, for a thinner consistency.

Candied Orange Rose

  1 cup granulated sugar
  1 cup water
  1 orange

1. Combine sugar and water in medium saucepan. Bring to a boil over medium-high heat, stirring occasionally.

2. Meanwhile, thinly peel orange with sharp knife, leaving as much membrane on orange as possible.

3. Carefully roll up peel, starting at one short end; secure with wooden pick.

4. Place on slotted spoon; add to hot sugar syrup.

5. Reduce heat to low; simmer 5 to 10 minutes or until orange rind turns translucent. Remove from syrup; place on waxed paper-lined cookie sheet to cool. Remove wooden pick.

Step 10. Spreading layers with marmalade.

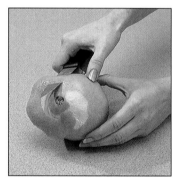

Candied Orange Rose: Step 2. Peeling orange.

Candied Orange Rose: Step 4. Adding rose to hot sugar syrup.

Caramel-Butter Pecan Cake

1 cup shortening
2 cups granulated sugar
4 eggs
3 cups sifted cake flour
2½ teaspoons baking powder
½ teaspoon salt
1 cup milk
1 teaspoon vanilla
1 teaspoon almond extract
   Caramel Filling (page 80)
   Buttercream Frosting
      (page 80)
¼ cup chopped pecans

1. Preheat oven to 350°F. Grease and flour three 9-inch round cake pans. (Technique on page 53.)

2. Beat together shortening and sugar in large bowl with electric mixer at medium speed until light and fluffy.

3. Add eggs, 1 at a time, beating well after each addition.

4. Sift together dry ingredients. Add to sugar mixture alternately with milk, beating well after each addition. Blend in vanilla and almond extract. Pour evenly into prepared pans.

5. Bake 20 to 25 minutes or until wooden pick inserted in centers comes out clean. Cool layers in pans on wire racks 10 minutes. Loosen edge of cake with knife or flexible metal spatula. Using oven mitts or hot pads, place wire cooling rack on top of cake in pan. Turn cake and pan over so wire rack is on bottom. Gently shake cake to release from pan. Remove pan. Repeat with remaining cake layers. Cool layers completely.

6. Gently brush loose crumbs off tops and sides of cake layers with pastry brush or hands. Prepare Caramel Filling. To assemble, spread tops of layers with filling; stack on cake plate.

7. Prepare Buttercream Frosting. To make basketweave design on side of cake, spoon ¼ to ⅓ of the frosting into pastry bag fitted with ridged decorator tip. Make vertical strips at 2-inch intervals around side of cake.

continued on page 80

Step 5. Removing cake layer to rack to cool.

Step 6. Spreading top of cake layer with Caramel Filling.

Step 7. Making vertical strips around side of cake.

Caramel-Butter Pecan Cake, continued

8. Make horizontal strip around side of cake, just below top edge. Repeat halfway down side of cake.

9. Repeat step 7, making one new strip at a point halfway between each of the strips made in step 7. (Continue to refill pastry tube with additional frosting as necessary.)

10. Make short horizontal strips, each at a point halfway between the horizontal strips made in step 8 and also at bottom of cake. Each short strip starts at the edge of one vertical strip, crosses over next vertical strip, and ends at edge of next vertical strip.

11. Replace ridged decorator tip with star tip. Pipe any remaining frosting around top of cake. Sprinkle with pecans.   *Makes one 3-layer cake*

Caramel Filling

3 cups granulated sugar, divided
³/₄ cup milk
1 egg, beaten
 Dash of salt
¹/₂ cup (1 stick) butter, softened

1. Place ¹/₂ cup granulated sugar in large heavy saucepan. Cook over medium heat, stirring constantly, until sugar is light golden brown.

2. Combine remaining 2¹/₂ cups granulated sugar, milk, egg and salt in medium bowl; stir in butter. Add to caramelized sugar.

3. Cook over medium heat, stirring occasionally, until candy thermometer registers 230°F (15 to 20 minutes); cool 5 minutes. Stir with wooden spoon until well blended and thickened.

Buttercream Frosting

¹/₃ cup (²/₃ stick) butter, softened
3 cups sifted powdered sugar
2 tablespoons half-and-half
¹/₂ teaspoon vanilla

1. Beat butter in large bowl with electric mixer at medium speed until creamy.

2. Gradually add powdered sugar alternately with half-and-half, beating until light and fluffy. Add additional 1 tablespoon half-and-half if necessary for desired consistency. Stir in vanilla.

Step 8. Making horizontal strips around side of cake.

Step 9. Making additional vertical strips.

Step 10. Making short horizontal strips.

Brandy-Pecan Corn Meal Cake

1 cup (2 sticks) margarine, softened
1¼ cups granulated sugar
¾ cup packed brown sugar
5 eggs
1 cup sour cream
½ cup brandy
2¼ cups all-purpose flour
½ cup Quaker® Enriched Corn Meal
2 teaspoons baking powder
1 teaspoon salt (optional)
1 teaspoon ground cinnamon
½ teaspoon ground nutmeg
1½ cups chopped pecans
Brandy Glaze (recipe follows)
Pecan halves for garnish

1. Preheat oven to 325°F. Generously grease and flour 10-inch fluted tube or tube pan. (Technique on page 53.)

2. Beat together margarine and sugars in large bowl with electric mixer at medium speed until light and fluffy. Add eggs, 1 at a time, beating well after each addition. Blend in sour cream and brandy.

3. Sift together dry ingredients. Add to margarine mixture, mixing until well blended. Stir in pecans. Pour into prepared pan, spreading evenly to edges.

4. Bake 65 to 70 minutes or until wooden pick inserted in center comes out clean. (Surface will appear slightly wet in center.)

5. Cool cake in pan on wire rack 10 minutes. Loosen edges and remove to rack to cool completely.

6. Prepare Brandy Glaze. Drizzle over cake. Garnish, if desired. Store tightly covered.

Makes one 10-inch tube cake

Step 4. Testing doneness with wooden pick.

Step 6. Drizzling Brandy Glaze over cake.

Brandy Glaze

2 tablespoons margarine
1 cup sifted powdered sugar
1 to 2 teaspoons brandy
4 to 5 teaspoons milk

1. Heat margarine in medium saucepan over medium heat until melted and golden brown; cool slightly.

2. Add powdered sugar, brandy and milk; beat until smooth.

Champion Pumpkin Cake

3/4 cup shortening
1 1/2 cups granulated sugar
3 eggs
1 1/2 cups solid-pack pumpkin
1 cup buttermilk
2 3/4 cups all-purpose flour
1 tablespoon baking powder
1 1/2 teaspoons baking soda
1/2 teaspoon salt
1 teaspoon ground cinnamon
1/4 teaspoon ground allspice
1/4 teaspoon ground nutmeg
1/8 teaspoon ground ginger
1/8 teaspoon pumpkin pie spice
Snow Frosting (recipe follows)

1. Preheat oven to 350°F. Grease and flour two 9-inch round cake pans. (Technique on page 53).

2. Beat shortening and granulated sugar in large bowl with electric mixer at medium speed until light and fluffy. Add eggs, 1 at a time, beating after each addition. Add pumpkin and buttermilk; beat well.

3. Sift together remaining dry ingredients; add to shortening mixture. Beat well. Pour evenly into prepared pans.

4. Bake 40 to 45 minutes or until wooden pick inserted in centers comes out clean. Cool in pans on wire racks 10 minutes. Loosen edges and remove to racks to cool completely. (Technique on page 12.)

5. Gently brush loose crumbs off tops and sides of cake layers with pastry brush or hands. Fill and frost with Snow Frosting.

Makes one 2-layer cake

Snow Frosting

1/2 cup shortening
1/2 cup (1 stick) butter, softened
2 egg whites*
1 teaspoon vanilla
4 cups sifted powdered sugar

*Use clean, uncracked eggs.

1. Beat together shortening and butter in large bowl with electric mixer at medium speed.

2. Add egg whites and vanilla; mix well. Gradually add powdered sugar, beating well.

Step 1. Flouring the pan.

Step 2. Adding eggs.

Step 3. Pouring batter into pans.

Kansas Kids' Cake

3/4 **cup honey**
1/2 **cup (1 stick) butter, softened**
1/4 **cup peanut butter**
2 **eggs**
1 **teaspoon vanilla**
1 **cup all-purpose flour**
1 **cup whole wheat flour**
1 1/2 **teaspoons baking powder**
3/4 **teaspoon baking soda**
1/2 **teaspoon salt**
3/4 **cup buttermilk**
Chunky Topping (recipe follows)

1. Preheat oven to 350°F. Grease 13×9-inch baking pan with small amount of shortening. Add 4 to 5 teaspoons flour to pan. Gently tap side to evenly coat bottom and side with flour. Invert pan and gently tap bottom to remove excess flour.

2. Beat together honey, butter and peanut butter in large bowl with electric mixer at medium speed until well blended. Blend in eggs and vanilla.

3. Sift together flours, baking powder, baking soda and salt; add to butter mixture alternately with buttermilk, beating well after each addition. Pour into prepared pan.

4. Prepare Chunky Topping; crumble over batter.

5. Bake 25 to 30 minutes or until wooden pick inserted in center comes out clean. Serve warm or at room temperature.

Makes one 13×9-inch cake

Chunky Topping

3/4 **cup sugar**
1/2 **cup peanut butter**
2 **tablespoons all-purpose flour**
1 **cup semisweet chocolate chips**

Combine sugar, peanut butter and flour in medium bowl, mixing until well blended. Stir in chocolate chips.

Step 2. Beating together honey, butter and peanut butter.

Step 4. Crumbling Topping over batter.

Step 5. Testing for doneness with wooden pick.

Turtle Pecan Cheesecake

8 ounces chocolate wafer cookies
  or vanilla wafers
¼ cup (½ stick) butter, melted
2½ packages (20 ounces total)
  cream cheese, softened
1 cup sugar
1½ tablespoons all-purpose flour
¼ teaspoon salt
1 teaspoon vanilla
3 eggs
2 tablespoons whipping cream
  Caramel Topping
  (recipe follows)
  Chocolate Topping
  (recipe follows)
1 cup chopped toasted pecans
  (technique on page 66)

1. Preheat oven to 450°F.

2. Place cookies in resealable plastic bag. Squeeze out excess air; seal bag tightly. Roll over cookies with rolling pin until finely crushed.

3. Combine cookie crumbs and butter; press onto bottom of 9-inch springform pan.

4. Beat cream cheese in large bowl with electric mixer at medium speed until creamy. Add sugar, flour, salt and vanilla; mix well. Add eggs, 1 at a time, beating well after each addition. Blend in cream. Pour over crust. Bake 10 minutes.

5. *Reduce oven temperature to 200°F.* Continue baking 35 to 40 minutes or until set. Loosen cake from rim of pan; remove rim. Cool.

6. Prepare Caramel Topping and Chocolate Topping. Drizzle toppings over cheesecake. Refrigerate cheesecake. Sprinkle with pecans.

Makes one 9-inch cheesecake

Step 2. Crushing cookies with rolling pin.

Step 4. Adding eggs.

Caramel Topping

½ (14-ounce) bag caramels
⅓ cup whipping cream

Combine ingredients in small saucepan; stir over low heat until smooth.

Chocolate Topping

4 ounces sweet baking chocolate
1 teaspoon butter
2 tablespoons whipping cream

Combine ingredients in small saucepan; stir over low heat until smooth.

Step 6. Drizzling Chocolate Topping over cheesecake.

Apple Cheesecake

1 cup graham cracker crumbs
  Sugar
1 teaspoon ground cinnamon,
  divided
3 tablespoons margarine, melted
2 packages (8 ounces each)
  cream cheese, softened
2 eggs
½ teaspoon vanilla
4 cups peeled, thin apple slices
  (about 2½ pounds apples)
½ cup chopped pecans

1. Preheat oven to 350°F.

2. Combine crumbs, 3 tablespoons sugar, ½ teaspoon cinnamon and margarine in small bowl; mix well. Press onto bottom and up side of 9-inch pie plate.

3. Bake crust 10 minutes.

4. Beat together cream cheese and ½ cup sugar in large bowl with electric mixer at medium speed until well blended. Add eggs, 1 at a time, beating well after each addition. Blend in vanilla; pour into crust.

5. Combine ⅓ cup sugar and remaining ½ teaspoon cinnamon in large bowl. Add apples; toss gently to coat.

6. Spoon apple mixture over cream cheese mixture.

7. Sprinkle with pecans.

8. Bake 1 hour and 10 minutes or until set. Cool completely before serving. Refrigerate.

Makes one 9-inch cheesecake

Step 2. Pressing crumb mixture onto bottom of pie plate.

Step 6. Spooning apple mixture over cream cheese mixture.

Step 7. Sprinkling with pecans.

Orange Cappuccino Cheesecake

1½ cups finely chopped nuts
1 cup *plus* 2 tablespoons sugar, divided
3 tablespoons butter, melted
4 packages (8 ounces each) cream cheese, softened
3 tablespoons all-purpose flour
4 eggs
1 cup sour cream
1 tablespoon instant coffee powder
¼ teaspoon ground cinnamon
¼ cup orange juice
1 teaspoon grated orange peel
Cinnamon sugar, whipped cream and additional grated orange peel for garnish

1. Preheat oven to 325°F.

2. Combine nuts, 2 tablespoons sugar and butter in medium bowl; mix well. Press onto bottom of 9-inch springform pan.

3. Bake 10 minutes. Remove from oven. *Increase oven temperature to 450°F.*

4. Beat together cream cheese, remaining 1 cup sugar and flour in large bowl with electric mixer at medium speed until well blended. Add eggs, 1 at a time, beating well after each addition. Blend in sour cream.

5. Add coffee powder and cinnamon to orange juice; stir until coffee is dissolved. Gradually add juice mixture with orange peel to cream cheese mixture, mixing until well blended. Pour over crust. Bake 10 minutes.

6. *Reduce oven temperature to 250°F.* Continue baking 1 hour.

7. Loosen cheesecake from rim of pan; cool 10 minutes. Sprinkle with cinnamon sugar. Lightly score top of cheesecake with sharp knife. Cool completely before removing rim of pan. Refrigerate.

8. Spoon desired amount of whipped cream into pastry tube; pipe around edge and in center of cheesecake. Sprinkle with orange peel, if desired.

Makes one 9-inch cheesecake

Step 2. Pressing nut mixture onto bottom of pan.

Step 7. Scoring top of cheesecake.

Step 8. Piping whipped cream around edge of cheesecake.

INDEX